What Are Forces and Motion?

Exploring Science with Hands-on Activities

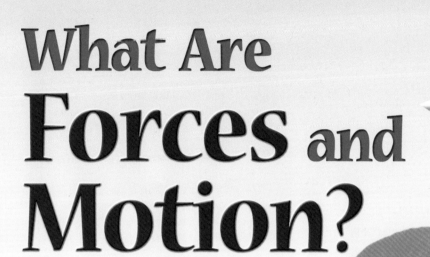

Richard and Louise Spilsbury

Enslow Elementary
an imprint of

E **Enslow Publishers, Inc.**
40 Industrial Road
Box 398
Berkeley Heights, NJ 07922
USA

http://www.enslow.com

Enslow Elementary, an imprint of Enslow Publishers, Inc.

Enslow Elementary® is a registered trademark of Enslow Publishers, Inc.

This edition published in 2008 by Enslow Publishers, Inc.

Library of Congress Cataloging-in-Publication Data

Spilsbury, Richard, 1963-
    What are forces and motion? : exploring science with hands-on activities / Richard and Louise Spilsbury.
        p. cm. —   (In touch with basic science)
    Summary: "An introduction for third and fourth grades on the properties of force and motion"—Provided by publisher.
    Includes bibliographical references and index.
    ISBN-13: 978-0-7660-3095-4
    ISBN-10: 0-7660-3095-4
    1. Force and energy—Experiments—Juvenile literature.
2. Motion—Experiments—Juvenile literature. 3. Science—Experiments—Juvenile literature. 4. Science—Study and teaching—Activity programs—Juvenile literature.
I. Spilsbury, Louise. II. Title.
    QC73.4.S67 2008
    531'.6078—dc22

                    2007024517

Printed in the United States of America

10 9 8 7 6 5 4 3 2 1

For The Brown Reference Group plc
Project Editor: Sarah Eason
Designer: Paul Myerscough
Picture Researcher: Maria Joannou
Managing Editor: Bridget Giles
Editorial Director: Lindsey Lowe
Production Director: Alastair Gourlay
Children's Publisher: Anne O'Daly

Photographic and Illustration Credits: Illustrations by Geoff Ward. Model Photography by Tudor Photography. Additional photographs from Dreamstime, p.18; NASA, p. 4; Shutterstock, pp. 8, 10, 27; US Department of Defense, p. 22.

Cover Photo: Tudor Photography

contents

FORCES AND MOTION

A force can make an object change its shape or motion (the way it moves). For instance, when you pull an elastic band you use a force to stretch it. A huge space shuttle can only lift off into space because its engines create a powerful force called thrust.

Newton's Laws

In 1686 English scientist Isaac Newton figured out three "laws of motion," which help explain how everything moves.

The First Law

Without force an object will either stay still, or keep moving in the same direction and speed as it was before the force occurred. So, a soccer ball stays still until it is kicked. Then the force of the kick moves it forward. The ball would keep moving if other forces did not act on it. The forces of friction and gravity make the ball slow down and stop.

CLOSE-UP

MOTION IN ACTION

Two pairs of forces are at work when an airplane zooms across the sky: gravity and lift, and thrust and drag.

● Lift pushes things upward. The shape of a plane's wing creates lift as air rushes over the wing.

● The plane's engine creates thrust to move the plane forward. Thrust must overcome drag for the plane to fly.

● Drag acts like friction to slow things down when they move through air or water.

● Gravity pulls everything toward Earth. To fly, a plane must create enough lift to overcome gravity.

◀ *A space shuttle is able to lift off because of the thrust created by a huge blast of burning fuel from its tanks.*

The Second Law

Force can slow down, speed up, or change the direction of an object. If a lot of force is used to kick a ball, it will move farther and faster than if less force were used.

The Third Law

Forces work in pairs. If one force acts on an object, an opposite force pushes back. For instance, the force of lift works against the force of gravity to push an airplane into the air.

Make a Jet-Ski

*How do Newton's laws work
in practice? Try this experiment
to find out.*

You will need
- 3 inch (7.5 cm) plastic tube or straw that can bend without breaking
- rubber stopper with a hole (or ask an adult to make a hole in a cork) • small, flat piece of Styrofoam™ • small balloon
- bathtub or wading pool filled with water • paper clip • large balloon

1 Push one end of the tube into the rubber stopper. Push the other end of the tube through one end of the Styrofoam tray.

2 Blow up a small balloon. Do not tie the end. Hold it together by pinching the end or by putting a paper clip on it.

WHAT HAPPENED?

Air shot backward out of the balloon. This pushed the jet-ski forward. That is an example of Newton's third law.

The jet-ski kept on moving after the balloon ran out of air, which is an example of Newton's first law.

The jet-ski slowed down and stopped because of drag. That is also an example of Newton's first law.

3 Stretch the mouth of the balloon over the rubber stopper. The end of the balloon should still be held together.

4 Rest your jet-ski on the water in a bathtub or wading pool, and point the end of the balloon backward. Take off the paper clip and release the balloon so air shoots out. How far does your jet-ski travel?

Try this!

How far will your jet-ski travel when you use a large balloon? Why does that make a difference? Which of Newton's laws explains this?

FORCES AND MACHINES

Machines make it easier to do work.
If a force moves or changes something, work
has been done. All machines use forces. It is
easy to see forces at work in simple machines,
such as ramps, screws, levers, and pulleys.

Raising Ramps

A ramp is a sloping surface. Ramps make it easier to lift
objects because less force is needed. Imagine trying to push
a heavy shopping cart over a curb onto
a sidewalk. Now imagine how much
easier it would be to push the
cart up a sloping ramp
onto the sidewalk.
The cart must be
pushed farther to get
it over the curb using
a ramp, but less force
is needed to push it.

Screws

Only a little force is needed to turn the handle of a screwdriver, but the screw moves forward with a greater force. Although a screwdriver must be turned many times to move a screw a little way, less effort or force is used to make each turn of the screw than if the screw were pushed straight in.

◀ *The ramp to this truck makes it easier to move heavy objects.*

turning motion

forward motion

CLOSE-UP

RAMPS AND SCREWS

Less force is needed to push a weight up a ramp than to lift it. However, the weight must be moved a greater distance when a ramp is used than if the weight were simply lifted.

pushing force

lifting force

A screw works in a similar way to a ramp. Look closely at a screw and you will see a small, narrow ramp that winds all the way around the screw. The screw changes the turning motion of the screwdriver handle into a forward pushing motion. This motion pushes the screw into a surface.

9

Levers

Some machines, such as levers, make it easier to lift heavy objects. Levers work best when they are placed over an object that serves as a fulcrum. Levers pivot or tilt around the fulcrum point.

You could use a lever to help you lift an object, such as a big rock, in the following way.

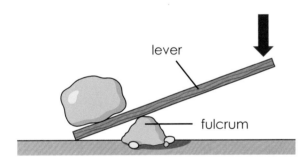

1. Place a stick (the lever) under the rock. Place another rock (the fulcrum) under the stick, making sure it is near the big rock.
2. Push down on the long end of the stick. The big, downward movement of the lever at this end lifts the big rock at the other.

You can see levers at work in scissors, some weighing scales, and claw hammers, which are used to pull nails out of wood.

▲ *Cranes act as a lever to lift and move loads.*

CLOSE-UP

EFFORT AND LOAD

When a rope passes over one pulley, it changes the direction of the force being used to lift a load.

When a rope runs through two pulleys, the pulleys can increase the pulling force and reduce the effort needed to lift a load.

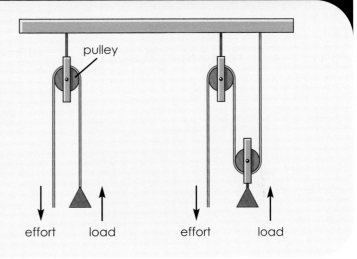

Pulleys

A pulley works with a wheel. When a rope passes over one wheel, it changes the direction of the force being used. When the rope is pulled down, the weight goes up. A pulley changes a *pulling* force into a *lifting* force. That helps someone to move a heavy load. People use pulleys to raise a flag up a flagpole, hoist a sail, or pull up a blind.

11

Ramp It Up!

How much force is needed to lift a load? Follow the steps to find out.

1 Ask an adult to make a small hole in the film canister lid with the hole punch. Use a pencil to help you thread the elastic through the hole, and tie a knot to keep the elastic from slipping out.

SAFETY TIP

An adult should make the holes in the canister lid.

2 Put the coins in the canister, then put on the lid.

You will need

- hole punch • film canister • rubber bands or piece of elastic • coins or metal nuts • ruler • books • wooden board or piece of plastic 2 feet (60 cm) long

3 Measure the elastic from the top of the canister to the end to see how long the elastic is when it is not stretched.

WHAT HAPPENED?

When a force is spread over a longer distance, a smaller force is needed to lift a load. The load traveled farther when it was pulled up the ramp, but less force was needed to move the load. That is why the elastic stretched less when you used the ramp.

4 Use the elastic to lift the canister to the height of a stack of books. Ask someone to measure how long the elastic is when the canister is at the same height as the top of the books.

5 Make a ramp using the board and the books. Use the elastic to slowly pull the canister to the top of the ramp. Measure the length of the elastic again. What do you discover?

Try this!

Try making the angle of your ramp steeper. How does this affect your results? Sprinkle talcum powder or oil on the ramp before pulling up the load. How does this affect your results?

13

Lever It Up!

Can a heavy weight be lifted by a smaller weight? Try this activity to find out.

You will need
- Two 12-inch (30-cm) rulers • 24 toothpicks
- 4 heavy books • 2 film canisters
- 6 same-size coins or metal nuts
- modeling clay

1 Tape a toothpick to each side of every 1-inch (2.5-cm) mark on a ruler.

2 Put both ends of the other ruler between two heavy books. Leave about 10 inches (25 cm) of the ruler uncovered between the books.

3 Break off two, same-size pieces of modeling clay. Put these on the bottom of the film canisters. Press one canister onto each end of the marked ruler, on the side without the toothpicks.

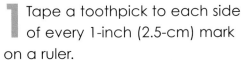

4 Put two coins or nuts in one of the canisters and four in the other. Rest your lever ruler across the middle of the ruler that is between the two books. Move the lever ruler as necessary until it balances.

5 Write down the position of the fulcrum (the point where the rulers touch). Write down the distances between the fulcrum and the weights (the canisters). Move the lever ruler up one toothpick notch (1 inch). What happens? Keep moving the lever up one toothpick notch at a time and record what happens.

WHAT HAPPENED?

Your results should show that as the distance from the fulcrum to the heavier weight became shorter, the weight became easier to lift. The smaller weight could then lift the heavier weight because the lever had become longer. Although the lever moved farther, less force was needed to push it. A longer lever can lift a greater weight, which is why the lighter weight was able to lift the heavier weight.

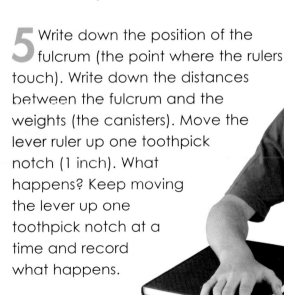

Pull It Up!

Does a pulley change a force?
Follow the steps to find out.

You will need

- pencil • thick cardboard • glue • 2 glasses of the same size • 1 smaller glass • hole punch • string • wooden dowel • 2 chairs • same-size coins or metal nuts • 2 plastic cups

1 Draw around the three glasses to make three cardboard circles. Ask an adult to cut out the circles.

2 Glue together the cardboard circles, with the smallest in the middle. Put a book on top of them until the glue is dry. Ask an adult to make a hole in the middle of the card wheel. Push a pencil through the hole.

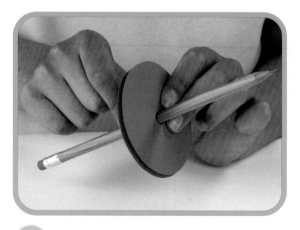

SAFETY TIP

Have an adult help you cut the cardboard and make a hole in it.

3 Make two holes in the tops of the plastic cups, at opposite sides. Tie a short piece of string between the holes in each cup.

WHAT HAPPENED?

When you added six coins to the second cup you created a downward pulling force. The pulley changed the direction of the downward force to a lifting force, which lifted the first cup.

4 Tie both ends of the pencil to the wooden dowel. Balance the dowel between two chairs, so that your pulley hangs in the air. Cut a long piece of string and hang it over the cardboard wheel.

5 Tie a cup to one end of the string and put six coins in it. Tie the other cup to the other end of the string. Add coins to this cup, until the first cup rises. How many coins are in each cup?

ENERGY

Everything needs energy to move or work. For example, people and animals get energy from food. Cars get energy from gasoline.

Kinetic Energy

The energy of movement is called kinetic energy. Kinetic energy is the energy an object has because it is moving.

The heavier an object is and the faster it moves, the more kinetic energy it has. When flying, a jumbo jet has far more kinetic energy than a flying bird or a bee because the jet is heavier and is moving faster.

Potential Energy

Energy can be stored in an object and then released. For example, when an archer pulls back and stretches a bow, the bow and string have a store of energy. Energy that is waiting to be used is called potential energy. When the archer releases the bow, the potential energy is released.

CLOSE-UP

GOING UP AND DOWN

If you throw a ball into the air, the balance between kinetic and potential energy changes. As the ball leaves your hands it has kinetic energy. When it starts to rise, its kinetic energy changes into potential energy. The ball continues to rise until all its kinetic energy has changed into potential energy. The ball then begins to fall back to the ground, and its potential energy changes into kinetic energy again.

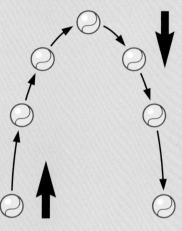

● Potential energy changes into kinetic energy.

● Kinetic energy changes into potential energy.

◀ *When an archer lets go of the bow, the potential energy in the stretched bow and string is converted to kinetic energy in the arrow.*

Changing Energy

Energy never disappears, and it cannot be created or destroyed. Energy simply changes from one kind of energy into another. When an arrow is fired from a bow, potential energy changes into kinetic energy. When the arrow is released, friction between the bow and the air changes some of the kinetic energy into heat energy.

Racing Tanks

How do potential and kinetic energy make things move? Follow the activity to find out.

1 Ask an adult to carefully cut off a ¼ inch (0.6 cm) piece from the bottom of the candle.

SAFETY TIP

Ask an adult to make all cuts in the candle for you.

2 Ask an adult to make a small hole in the center of your piece of candle. Have them cut a groove into one side. This should be big enough to hold a toothpick.

You will need
- empty spool • candle • 2 toothpicks
- knife • small rubber band

3 Put the rubber band through the spool. One end of the rubber band should stick out at each end of the spool. Now pull one end of the rubber band through the candle hole. Put a toothpick through that end of the rubber band.

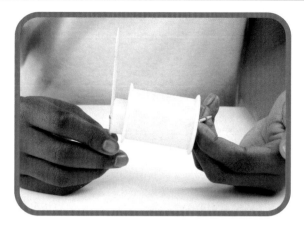

4 Use half a toothpick to hold the remaining end of the rubber band in place. You have made a tank!

5 Twist the rubber band by turning the long toothpick. This will wind up your tank. What happens? Try racing your tank against a friend's!

WHAT HAPPENED?

When you wound up and tightened the rubber band, a store of potential energy was created inside the band. The potential energy changed into kinetic energy when you released the elastic band. The energy made the tank move along as the rubber band unwound.

Try this!

Test your tank on other surfaces, such as carpet, sandpaper, and a very smooth table. Why does it move more slowly on rougher surfaces? What happens to the tank's kinetic energy?

FLOATING AND SINKING

Objects can feel lighter when they are in water because the force of the water pushes upward against them. This force makes some objects float on the surface of water—but why do other objects sink?

Buoyant Force

When an object is lowered into water, it displaces (pushes aside) some of the water. That is why the water level rises when you get into a bathtub. The water pushes upward against the object, and may even hold it up. The pushing force of a liquid such as water is called buoyant force.

The buoyant force is equal to the weight of liquid displaced by the object. The bigger an object is, the more liquid it displaces, and the greater the buoyant force is.

▼ *Submarine tanks, called ballast tanks, are filled with air to make the submarine float. The tanks are filled with water to make the submarine sink.*

Density

Have you ever noticed that two objects can take up the same amount of space, but one may be heavier than the other? The one that has more mass—more matter—in the same amount of space is denser. Objects can only float in water if they have a lower density than the water. However, any material can float if its shape is changed so that it displaces enough water to create a buoyant force.

CLOSE-UP

FLOATING IRON

An iron ship floats because ships are designed to displace a lot of water. They also contain many rooms and spaces filled with air. The air inside these spaces makes the ship light in relation to its size. The ship is less dense than water, which is why it floats.

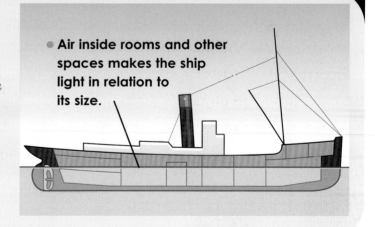

Air inside rooms and other spaces makes the ship light in relation to its size.

Pen-Cap Diver

How does changing the density of an object change how it behaves in water? Try this experiment to find out.

You will need
- plastic cap from ballpoint pen
- modeling clay • water
- glass • large bottle of water

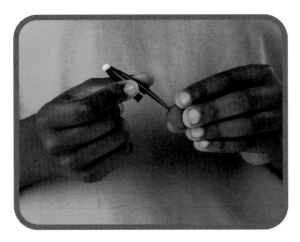

1 If your pen cap has a tiny hole at the top, block it with a small piece of modeling clay. Then put a bigger piece of clay around the end of the pen cap's clip. Congratulations—you have made a pen-cap diver!

2 Put the cap in a glass of water to see if it will float.

3 Add or remove tiny pieces of clay from the pen's clip until your diver floats in the glass of water.

4 Fill the plastic bottle with water, almost to the top. Put the pen-cap diver in the bottle and screw on the lid.

5 Grip the bottle with both hands. Squeeze it firmly. What happens to the diver? Let go of the bottle again. What happens to the diver now?

WHAT HAPPENED?

The pen cap floated because it had a bubble of air in its tip. This bubble made the cap less dense than the water. If you put too much modeling clay on the pen cap, it sank. That was because the density of the diver increased.

When you squeezed the bottle, the water in the bottle was compressed. This, in turn, compressed the air inside the pen cap, which made the air denser. This change in density made the pen-cap diver sink.

BUILDING WITH FORCES

People who make a structure must take forces into account. There are several kinds of bridges, including suspension, arch, and beam bridges. Forces act on these bridges in different ways.

Beam Bridges

Beam bridges are very simple. They have a flat, solid surface that is supported at both ends where the bridge meets the ground.

The weight of a load, such as a vehicle or a person, in the middle of a beam bridge creates a downward pushing force. The farther apart the bridge's supports are, the less weight the bridge can support. That is why beam bridges are never very long.

CLOSE-UP

BRIDGES AND FORCES

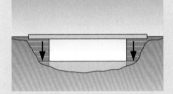

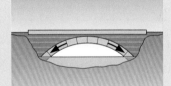

- If the downward force that acts on a beam bridge is too great it can bend and crack the bridge.

- The downward force of a load spreads outward to the sides of an arch bridge and down into the ground.

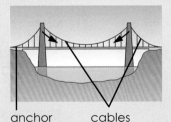

anchor   cables

- The downward force of a load pulls on and tightens the cables of a suspension bridge. The cables then pull on strong concrete anchors on the land on either side of the bridge.

Arch Bridges

Some bridges are supported underneath by a round arch. When a weight pushes down on the middle of an arch bridge, the force is carried to the bridge's sides. The force is then carried downward, to the ground at either end of the bridge. That is why arch bridges can usually support more weight than beam bridges.

Suspension Bridges

Suspension bridges hang from two huge cables that are held up by tall towers. The cables run to the land on either side of the bridge. Smaller cables run vertically from the main cables to the bridge deck.

When a weight pushes down on the deck of a suspension bridge, it creates a pulling force that acts on the small vertical cables. These cables pull on the main cables, and the force is transferred to the anchors in the ground at the end of the main cables.

▼ *When it was completed in 1937, the Golden Gate Bridge in San Francisco was the largest suspension bridge in the world.*

Buckling Bridges

*Can a bridge hold more weight
when it is supported by an arch?
Try this activity to find out.*

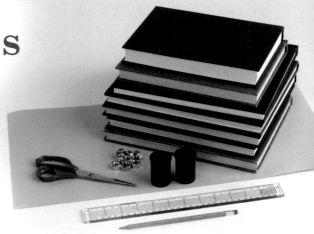

1 Use the ruler to draw a rectangle 22 inches (55 cm) long and 2 inches (5 cm) wide on the cardboard.

2 Have an adult cut out the cardboard strip. Mark the halfway point on the strip with a ruler.

You will need

- ruler • pencil • thick cardboard
- scissors • 2 piles of heavy books
- film canisters • coins or metal nuts to use as weights

3 Place your two piles of books 18 inches (45 cm) apart on the table. Make a bridge between them with the cardboard strip. Place one book on top of each pile of books. That will hold the strip in place.

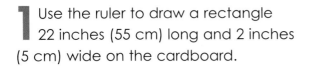

SAFETY TIP

Ask an adult to help you cut the cardboard.

4 Put the canister on the halfway point of the cardboard strip. Put a coin or metal nut in the canister. Use the ruler to measure the distance from the table to the center of the bridge. Keep adding weights and taking measurements until the bridge touches the table.

5 Now cut a strip of cardboard 30 inches (76 cm) long. Put one end under each pile of books. Bend the strip of cardboard upward to make an arch. Try the test in step 4 again. What happens?

WHAT HAPPENED?

The beam bridge was supported only at its ends, which is why it bent easily. When the weight pressed down on the arch, the downward force spread across the arch and transferred to the ground. That is why the bridge could hold more weight when it was supported by the arch.

Try this!

Make a graph from your results. Record the number of weights in the canister on the horizontal axis. Record how much space is between the table and the bridge on the vertical axis. Can you think of another way to make your beam bridge even stronger?

GLOSSARY

buoyant force—Force that pushes an object upward in water.

density—Describes how much mass something has in relation to its size.

displace—To take the place of, or to move. When an object is put into water, it displaces a certain amount of the water.

effort—The amount of force exerted by a person or machine to make something move or change.

force—Something that can change an object's motion or shape.

friction—A force that lessens the movement of matter that is in contact with other matter.

fulcrum—The point at which a lever pivots or tilts. A lever can rest on an object that serves as a fulcrum.

kinetic energy—Energy related to the motion of an object.

lever—A bar or other similar item that pivots or tilts around a fulcrum.

load—Weight of an object being moved.

machine—An item or tool that reduces the effort required to do work.

motion—Movement, or the way something moves.

potential energy—Energy stored in an object.

pulley—A wheel with a grooved rim through which a rope can pass to change the direction of the force used to pull the rope.

ramp—A sloping surface that reduces the effort needed to move something.

screw—A simple machine with a spiral of ridges. The ridges allow the screw to be moved forward into another material by turning it, with less effort than would be required to push it.

work—The use of force to move or change something.